I0815066

GEORGE W. BUSH

PIVOTAL PRESIDENTS
Profiles in Leadership

GEORGE W. BUSH

Edited by Kenneth Zahensky

Published in 2018 by Britannica Educational Publishing (a trademark of Encyclopædia Britannica, Inc.) in association with The Rosen Publishing Group, Inc.
29 East 21st Street, New York, NY 10010

Distributed exclusively by Rosen Publishing.
To see additional Britannica Educational Publishing titles, go to rosenpublishing.com.

First Edition

Britannica Educational Publishing
J.E. Luebering: Executive Director, Core Editorial
Andrea R. Field: Managing Editor, Compton's by Britannica

Rosen Publishing
Kathy Kuhtz Campbell: Senior Editor
Nelson Sá: Art Director
Brian Garvey : Series Designer
Alison Hird: Book Layout
Cindy Reiman: Photography Manager
Bruce Donnola: Photo Researcher
Supplementary material by Kenneth Zahensky

Library of Congress Cataloging-in-Publication Data

Names: Zahensky, Kenneth, editor.
Title: George W. Bush / edited by Kenneth Zahensky.
Description: First edition. | New York: Britannica Educational Publishing in Association with Rosen Educational Services, 2018. | Series: Pivotal presidents: profiles in leadership | Includes bibliographical references and index.
Identifiers: LCCN 2015048863 | ISBN 9781680486292 (library bound)
Subjects: LCSH: Bush, George W. (George Walker), 1946—Juvenile literature. Presidents—United States—Biography—Juvenile literature. | United States—Politics and government—2001–2009—Juvenile literature.
Classification: LCC E903 .G463 2016 | DDC 972.931092—dc23
LC record available at http://lccn.loc.gov/2015048863

Manufactured in China

Photo credits: Cover, pp. 3 (portrait), 7 Eric Draper/The White House; cover, p. 3 (background) Brooks Kraft/Corbis Historical/Getty Images; cover, pp. 1, 3 (flag) © iStockphoto.com/spxChrome; pp. 11, 14 Handout/Hulton Archive/Getty Images; p. 12 Handout/KRT/Newscom; p. 16 White House Photo; p. 21 Shelly Katz/The LIFE Images Collection/Getty Images; pp. 24, 43 New York Daily News Archive/Getty Images; p. 26 Rhona Wise/AFP/Getty Images; p. 29 The White House/Hulton Archive/ Getty Images; p. 31 Tim Sloan/AFP/Getty Images; pp. 34, 62 Spencer Platt/Getty Images; p. 35 The White House/Getty Images; p. 38 George W. Bush Library/NARA; p. 45 Ramzi Haidar/AFP/Getty Images; p. 47 Johan Charles Van Boers/U.S. Department of Defense; p. 48 Mario Tama/Getty Images; p. 51 Bloomberg/Getty Images; pp. 52, 59 AFP/Getty Images; p. 55 David McNew/Getty Images; p. 58 Paul Morse/The White House; p. 61 John Moore/Getty Images; p. 64 Getty Images; interior pages flag Fedorov Oleksiy/Shutterstock.com

Table of Contents

Introduction

George W. Bush, the oldest son of former US president George H. W. Bush, emerged from the shadow of his famous father to be elected president himself in 2000. As a popular governor of Texas, Bush had won national attention as a so-called "new Republican" who combined traditional Republican Party values with a self-described "compassionate conservative" social outlook. In describing his philosophy, Bush explained:

> *"It is compassionate to actively help our fellow citizens in need. It is conservative to insist on responsibility and results. And with this hopeful approach, we will make a real difference in people's lives."*

Bush's combination of country-boy charisma and boundless enthusiasm eventually helped him win election as the country's forty-third chief executive. With his victory, he took his place alongside John Quincy Adams as the second son of a president also to serve in the office.

To reach the White House, however, Bush had to win one of the closest and most fiercely contested presidential elections in US history. The final popular vote totals put Bush behind

Family and Childhood

George Bush, posing here at the age of seven or eight, enjoyed playing baseball in his youth.

George Walker Bush was born in New Haven, Connecticut, on July 6, 1946, the grandson of former Connecticut senator Prescott Bush and the son of George Herbert Walker Bush and his wife, Barbara Bush. After graduating from Yale University, George H. W. Bush moved his family to Midland, Texas, where his son George spent his formative years while his father amassed a fortune in the booming oil industry.

Despite their wealth, the Bush family initially led a modest lifestyle typical of their small west Texas town. The oldest of six children, George

W. Bush would later recall that his experience as a child in Midland instilled in him a love of small-town life and an appreciation of traditional conservative values of family, community, and religion. Bush's genuinely happy childhood was marred by one episode of family tragedy when his younger sister Robin died of leukemia at the age of three in 1953.

Education

By his own admission, Bush never harbored a tremendous interest in book learning. Instead of reading and studying, he spent his youth playing baseball and other games.

Bush was head cheerleader during his senior year at Phillips Academy in Andover, Massachusetts. He had outstanding people skills at a young age and spearheaded pep rallies at the school.

He earned decent grades and a reputation in school as a bright but somewhat unruly child. Despite his inconsistency in school, Bush gained admittance to Phillips Academy in Andover, Massachusetts, one of the most prestigious preparatory schools in the country. His father had graduated from there.

Despite a mediocre academic record at Andover, Bush earned admittance to his father's and grandfather's alma mater, Yale University, in 1964. Although Bush compiled a lackluster academic record en route to graduating with a degree in history, he did hone remarkable talents for socializing and winning friends that would serve him well throughout his later political life.

Business, Marriage, and Politics

After leaving Yale in 1968, Bush returned to Texas, where he drifted through a number of towns, worked in a variety of jobs, and gained his first experience in politics. Soon after leaving college, he was accepted into the Texas Air National Guard as a pilot trainee, a post that made it unlikely that he would have to serve in the Vietnam War. In 1970, he was

Around 1970 Bush posed next to a jet during his service as a pilot in the Texas Air National Guard.

certified as a fighter pilot. That year he also worked as a campaign aide to his father, who unsuccessfully ran for the US Senate. Bush also applied for admission to the University of Texas law school but was rejected.

Despite apparently missing at least eight months of duty between May 1972 and May 1973, Bush was granted an early discharge in the fall of 1973 to attend business school at Harvard University. After earning a master's degree in 1975, Bush returned to his hometown of Midland, where he married Laura Welch, a former classmate from junior high school. Four years later, they had twin daughters, Barbara and Jenna.

Determined to make his own name as a businessman, Bush founded Bush Exploration, an oil and gas surveying company. In 1978, despite having achieved only modest success in the business world, he ran for an open seat in the US House of Representatives. He ran a surprisingly strong campaign in a mostly Democratic district, but he lost the election.

Business concerns occupied much of Bush's attention in the following years. A sharp drop in oil prices in the early 1980s hurt his fledgling company. In 1984, Bush merged his company with another firm, Spectrum

Corporation, but the downward spiral in the oil industry continued. Bush was forced to sell the failing oil company to Harken Energy Corporation in 1986. He received Harken stock, a job as a consultant to the company, and a seat on the company's board of directors.

The failure of Spectrum Corporation had a profound impact on Bush. During the time of his business troubles, Bush met Christian evangelical preacher Billy Graham at the Bush family estate in Kennebunkport, Maine. Following that meeting, Bush—who

The Bushes pose for a family photograph at their estate in Kennebunkport, Maine. George W. Bush, third from the right, sits in front of his father with his wife, Laura, and their daughter Barbara. Daughter Jenna stands behind her grandparents at the upper right.

Laura Welch Bush

Laura Lane Welch was born in Midland on November 4, 1946. Her parents placed a high priority on the education of their only child and fostered her interest in reading. She attended public schools in Midland and graduated from high school in 1964. After earning a bachelor's degree in elementary education from Southern Methodist University in 1968, she taught in public schools in Dallas and Houston. She received a master's degree in library science from the University of Texas in 1973 and later worked as a librarian in Austin.

Although George W. Bush and Laura Welch attended the same middle school for one year and even lived for a brief period in the same apartment complex in Houston, they did not meet until 1977. They were introduced by mutual friends at a barbecue. Three months later, on November 5, 1977, they married—but reportedly only after George agreed that Laura would never have to give a political speech on his behalf. Laura then resigned her job as a librarian and did volunteer work at a Dallas hospital. In 1981, she gave birth to twin daughters, Barbara and Jenna, who were named after their grandmothers.

After George was elected governor of Texas in 1994, Laura became a popular first lady, working to improve literacy and raising funds for public libraries. She also promoted breast cancer awareness and other women's health issues.

In 1999, George W. Bush announced his candidacy for the Republican presidential nomination. Although Laura Bush had earlier resisted giving public campaign speeches, she became an avid campaigner, even addressing the Republican National Convention in 2000. As first lady of the United States, she continued her focus on education, establishing a foundation to raise funds for libraries and organizing a national book fair featuring American authors.

was raised as an Episcopalian but converted to Methodism following his marriage—rededicated himself to Christianity. Known during his younger years for his fondness for partying and alcohol, Bush also resolved to quit drinking and devote himself more completely to his family life.

In 1987, Bush traveled to Washington, DC, to work as a high-level adviser on his father's campaign for the US presidency. Following his father's victory, Bush returned to Texas and settled in Dallas, where he received the largest break of his business career. In 1988, the owners of the Texas Rangers professional baseball team announced their intention to sell the team. Bush, a lifelong baseball fan, put together a coalition of local businessmen to purchase the team for $46 million. While Bush himself contributed just over $600,000, his fellow investors named him managing partner of the Rangers.

Bush's period with the Rangers provided him with his first unqualified business success. During his tenure, the Rangers became both a competitive team and a financial success. Moreover, Bush's high-profile position as managing partner made him a prominent figure throughout Texas.

CHAPTER 2

State and National Politics

Bush hoped to carry his newfound business success into the political realm by running for public office. He would go on to make his mark in state politics before moving on to the national level.

GOVERNORSHIP OF TEXAS

In 1994, Bush challenged the popular Democratic incumbent, Ann Richards, for the governorship of Texas. He emphasized such issues as reforming welfare, combating juvenile crime, and overhauling the state's school system. Buoyed in large part by a nationwide backlash against the Democratic Party for 1993 tax increases, Bush succeeded in upsetting Richards in the election. He was the first child of a US president to be elected a state governor.

As governor of Texas, Bush won accolades from his supporters for passing two large tax cuts, for reducing state spending, and for lowering the rate of juvenile and adult crime. He also oversaw an overhaul of the state's school system and curriculum and made the salaries and promotions of teachers and administrators contingent on their students' performance on standardized tests. In addition, Bush made a concerted effort to expand the base of the Republican Party by courting minority voters who traditionally backed the Democratic Party.

Bush called his moderate Republican outlook "compassionate conservatism"—a philosophy that purportedly combined the traditional Republican platform of tax cuts and reduced government spending with a more Democratic concern for social issues and the underprivileged. Opponents questioned the "compassionate" label, however, in light of some of Bush's policies. His administration increased the number of crimes for which juveniles could be sentenced to adult prisons and lowered to fourteen the age at which children could be tried as adults. Throughout his tenure, Bush received international attention for the frequent use of capital punishment in Texas relative to other states. He authorized the execution of more than 150 convicted criminals, a rate that far exceeded the national average.

Bush interacts with supporters while campaigning for governor of Texas in 1994. He went on to win 53 percent of the popular vote.

Reelection as Governor

Bush easily won reelection as governor in 1998 with a record 69 percent of the vote. He became the first Texas governor to win consecutive four-year terms. (In 1972, Texas voters had approved a referendum that extended the governor's term from two years to four.) On the same day Bush won reelection in Texas, his younger brother Jeb won the governorship of Florida. They became the first brothers to serve as governors at the same time since 1967, when Winthrop and Nelson Rockefeller served as governors of Arkansas and New York, respectively.

In 1999, Bush signed a law that deregulated the Texas electricity market. The law's goal was to increase competition in the state's power industry and decrease power rates for consumers. The law directed electric companies to purchase a certain amount of renewable energy, such as solar and wind power. It helped propel Texas as a leading producer of wind power.

Bush's popularity and political successes as governor made him an early front-runner in the 2000 presidential election. On June 12, 1999, Bush officially announced his candidacy for the Republican presidential nomination. Although he faced a stiff challenge from Senator John McCain of Arizona, Bush eventually emerged as the Republican candidate to oppose Vice President Al Gore, the Democratic Party's nominee, in the election.

The Presidential Election of 2000

During his campaign, Bush won praise from his supporters for attempting to expand the traditional base of the Republican Party by emphasizing a message of political inclusion for minority Americans. He called for sizable tax cuts for families in an effort to appeal to a broader cross section of the population. To shore up support among the core constituency of the Republican Party, Bush selected Dick Cheney as his vice presidential candidate. Cheney, who had served as secretary of defense during the administration of George H. W. Bush, was regarded as a talented politician with the type of faultless conservative credentials needed to balance Bush's more moderate views.

In the election of November 7, 2000, Bush won the popular vote in thirty states while Gore prevailed in twenty states and the District of Columbia. Bush swept the South and much of the Plains and Rocky Mountain regions, but Gore took the more populous states in the Northeast and on the West Coast along with some key states in the

Bush (*left*), the Republican presidential candidate, addresses supporters during a campaign trip through the Midwest in 2000. With him are his wife, Laura (*right*); his vice presidential running mate, Dick Cheney; and Cheney's wife, Lynne (*center*).

Midwest, leading to a remarkably tight contest in the electoral college. Eventually, the outcome of the election came to hinge on the state of Florida, with both candidates needing its twenty-five electoral votes to reach the threshold of 270 required to win.

The initial tally in Florida gave Bush a victory in the popular vote by about 1,800 votes out of some 6 million cast. An automatic machine recount, required by Florida law because of the narrow margin of victory, reduced Bush's lead to fewer than 1,000 votes four days after the election. The closeness

Bush v. Gore

The presidential election of 2000 was one of the tightest and most controversial contests in US history. Five weeks after the election, the presidency still was undecided, as some fifty individual lawsuits were filed concerning vote counts, recounts, and certification deadlines. The Florida Supreme Court ordered a statewide manual recount of about 45,000 "undervotes"—that is, ballots that machines recorded as not clearly expressing a presidential vote. The Bush campaign filed suit to stop the manual recounts, and the US Supreme Court agreed to hear the case.

On December 9, in a 5–4 decision, the US Supreme Court ruled in the case of *Bush v. Gore* that the manual recounts must stop. It also agreed to hear oral arguments from both parties. Bush's team asserted that the Florida Supreme Court had exceeded its authority by authorizing the recount of undervotes. Gore's team stated that the case, having already been decided at the state level, was not a matter for consideration at the federal level. The following day, in a 7–2 ruling, the US Supreme Court overturned the Florida decision, holding that the various methods and standards of the recount process violated the equal protection clause of the US Constitution. The court ruled 5–4 on the remedy of the matter, with the majority holding that the Florida Supreme Court's decision had created new election law—a right reserved for the state legislature—and that no recount could be held in time to satisfy a federal deadline for the selection of state electors.

The decision of the majority was heavily criticized by the minority. Dissenting justices wrote that the recount process, while flawed, should be allowed to proceed, on the grounds that constitutional protection of each vote should not be subject to a timeline. Particularly notable was Justice Ruth Bader Ginsburg's dissent, which she ended with "I dissent" rather than the traditional "I respectfully dissent." With the termination of the recount process, Florida's twenty-five electoral votes were awarded to Bush. Gore officially conceded on December 13 and stated in a televised address, "While I strongly disagree with the court's decision, I accept it."

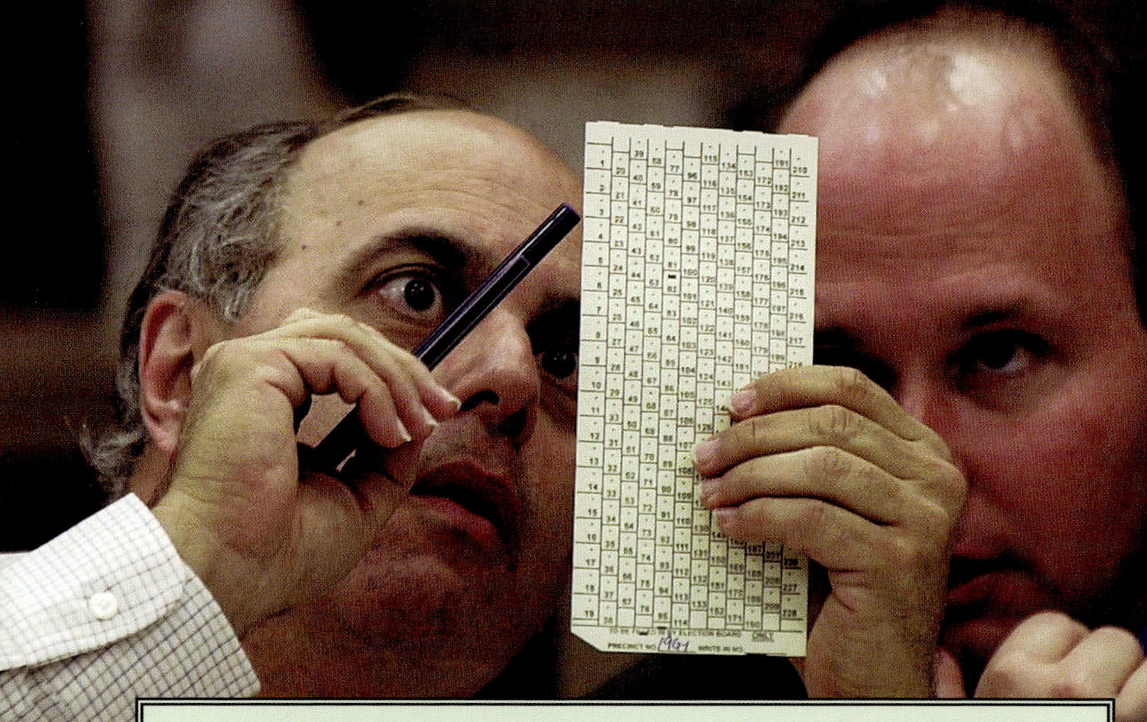

Voting officials in Ft. Lauderdale, Florida, review a ballot on November 23, 2000, during a manual recount of votes for the presidential election. The officials were trying to meet a Florida State Supreme Court deadline to accept hand-counted ballots for certification.

of the vote led to a drawn-out legal battle, with the Gore campaign requesting manual recounts in several heavily Democratic counties in which it was claimed that the use of outmoded machinery resulted in an exceptionally high number of disqualified ballots.

Over the following weeks, attorneys for both candidates argued before federal courts, the Florida Supreme Court, and eventually the US Supreme Court, with the Gore team pressing for recounts and the Bush camp seeking to prevent them. During this period,

Bush's lead fluctuated as a result of various recounts and the addition of absentee ballots. The first certification of the Florida vote, made one week after the election, gave Bush a 300-vote margin of victory; a revised certification two weeks later put Bush's lead officially at 537 votes.

After more than a month of legal wrangling, the US Supreme Court issued a split decision that reversed a Florida Supreme Court ruling and halted the recounts, preserving Bush's slight lead in the popular vote in Florida and in effect awarding him the state's decisive electoral votes. As he took office in January 2001, Bush had before him the task of governing a country deeply divided in its opinions concerning the legitimacy of his victory.

Chapter 3

Early Presidency

Bush was the first Republican president to enjoy a majority in both houses of Congress since Dwight D. Eisenhower in the 1950s. His initial task was to set up his administration and set his legislative agenda. Less than a year into his term, however, his presidency would be radically changed when the United States suffered the deadliest terrorist attacks on its soil in the country's history.

The Cabinet

In keeping with the selection of Dick Cheney as his vice president, Bush chose several of his father's most trusted advisers for his Cabinet. Among these loyal Bush supporters were two of the country's most distinguished African Americans, retired general Colin Powell and foreign policy expert Condoleezza Rice. Bush appointed Powell as secretary of state and Rice as national security adviser. He named Donald Rumsfeld as secretary of defense, a post Rumsfeld had held under President Gerald Ford. Bush's most controversial Cabinet appointment was John Ashcroft as attorney general. Ashcroft was narrowly confirmed by the Senate after facing intensive questioning by Democrats regarding his civil rights record and views on such issues as abortion rights.

President George W. Bush and Vice President Dick Cheney pose (*front row, center*) with Bush's Cabinet in the Oval Office of the White House in April 2001.

Legislative Initiatives

Taking advantage of the Republican majority in Congress, Bush proposed a $1.6 trillion tax-cut bill in February 2001. A compromise measure worth $1.35 billion was passed by Congress in June, despite Democratic objections that it unfairly benefited the wealthy. In the same month, however, control of the Senate formally passed to the Democrats after Republican senator James Jeffords of Vermont left his party to become an independent. Thereafter, many of Bush's domestic initiatives encountered significant resistance in the Senate.

The National Energy Policy Development Group, a task force headed by Vice President Dick Cheney, issued a report in May 2001. It called for increasing the production of fossil fuels and nuclear power in the country by opening more federal lands to mining and oil and gas exploration, extending tax credits and other subsidies to energy companies, and easing environmental regulations. In July, a coalition of nonprofit organizations filed suit to make public the secret deliberations of the task force and the identities of the groups it met with. (The case was decided in the administration's favor by the Supreme Court in June 2004.)

The Bush administration worked on legislation aimed at improving public schools. It hoped to enhance student performance through increased accountability for schools, school districts, and states. In December 2001, Congress passed the No Child Left Behind Act, and Bush signed it into law in January 2002.

A student speaks to President Bush during the signing of the No Child Left Behind Act in January 2002.

In foreign affairs, the Bush administration took steps that reduced the country's international commitments. It opposed international measures to control global warming, withdrew from the 1972 treaty on antiballistic missiles, and rejected the jurisdiction of the new International Criminal Court.

The No Child Left Behind Act

President Bush won bipartisan support in Congress for the No Child Left Behind Act (NCLB). It introduced significant changes in the curriculum of US public primary and secondary schools and increased federal regulation of state school systems. States were required to administer annual tests of the reading and mathematics skills of public school students and to demonstrate adequate progress toward raising the scores of all students to a level defined as "proficient" or higher by 2014. Teachers had to meet higher standards for certification. Schools that failed to meet their goals would be subject to gradually increasing sanctions, eventually including replacement of staff members or closure.

Supporters of NCLB cited its initial success in increasing the test scores of minority students, who historically performed at lower levels than white students. Critics, however, complained that the federal government was not providing enough funding to carry out the law's requirements and that it had violated the states' traditional control of education as provided for in the Constitution. They also said that the law actually eroded the quality of education by forcing schools to "teach to the test" or to lower standards of proficiency while neglecting other parts of the curriculum, such as history, social science, and art. In 2015, Bush's successor, President Barack Obama, signed into law the Every Student Succeeds Act, which repealed several of the most-unpopular provisions of NCLB.

The Terrorist Attacks

On September 11, 2001, Bush confronted a crisis that transformed his presidency. Terrorists hijacked four US commercial airplanes, deliberately crashing two of them into the twin towers of the World Trade Center in New York City and a third into the Department of Defense headquarters at the Pentagon building outside Washington, DC. The fourth plane crashed in a Pennsylvania field after passengers rebelled against the hijackers. Fearful for the safety of the president, who was in Florida when the day began, the Secret Service flew him to Air Force bases in Louisiana and Nebraska. By the time Bush returned to the White House that night, the World Trade Center was in ruins, one side of the Pentagon was seriously damaged, and some 3,000 people had died.

The Bush administration blamed the September 11 attacks on al-Qaeda, an Islamic extremist group led by Osama bin Laden (in a videotape in 2004, bin Laden acknowledged that he was responsible). The Taliban government of Afghanistan was accused of harboring bin Laden and his followers.

On September 11, 2001, terrorists hijacked two passenger airplanes and crashed them into the twin towers of the World Trade Center in New York City. A third hijacked plane was flown into the Pentagon near Washington, DC, and a fourth crashed in a Pennsylvania field.

After assembling an international military coalition, Bush ordered a massive bombing campaign against Afghanistan, which began on October 7, 2001. The US-led forces quickly toppled the Taliban government and routed al-Qaeda fighters, although bin Laden himself remained elusive (he was eventually killed in a raid by US forces in Pakistan in 2011). In the wake of the September 11 attacks and during the war in Afghanistan, Bush's public-approval ratings were the highest of his presidency, reaching 90 percent in some polls.

On September 14, 2001, President Bush speaks through a bullhorn to firefighters, police officers, and other emergency workers at the ruins of the World Trade Center, which became known as Ground Zero.

Domestic Security

Immediately after the September 11 attacks, domestic security and the threat of terrorism became the chief focus of the Bush administration and the top priority of government at every level. Declaring a global "war on terrorism," Bush announced that the country would not rest until "every terrorist group of global reach has been found, stopped, and defeated."

To coordinate the government's domestic response and to protect the country against further attacks, Bush created the Office of Homeland Security, which became a Cabinet-level department in 2003. He chose Governor Tom Ridge of Pennsylvania to head this department. The department was to ensure that federal, state, and local agencies worked together in their counterterrorism efforts.

In October 2001, the Bush administration introduced, and Congress quickly passed, the Uniting and Strengthening America by Providing Appropriate Tools Required to Intercept and Obstruct Terrorism Act (the USA PATRIOT Act). It gave the Federal Bureau of Investigation (FBI) and other

USA PATRIOT Act

The USA PATRIOT Act was passed by the US Congress in response to the September 11 terrorist attacks and signed into law by President Bush in October 2001. The law significantly expanded the search and surveillance powers of federal law-enforcement and intelligence agencies in pursuing suspected terrorists and in detaining them.

Some key provisions of the law consisted of amendments to the Wiretap Act, which had prohibited eavesdropping by the government on private face-to-face, telephone, and electronic communications except as authorized by court order in narrowly defined circumstances in cases of serious crimes. Sections 201 and 202 of the USA PATRIOT Act added computer and terrorist crimes to the list of serious offenses in reference to which law-enforcement officials could seek a court order to conduct eavesdropping. Section 209 established that voice mail was not entitled to the same protections that governed telephone conversations but only to the weaker safeguards applicable to telephone records and email stored with third parties (usually an internet service provider).

Section 216 permitted the use of trap-and-trace devices (which show all incoming numbers to a specific phone) and pen registers (which show outgoing numbers) to monitor electronic communications, understood to include email and internet browsing. Court orders for such surveillance did not require probable cause—a showing of facts that would lead a reasonable person to believe that the surveillance would be likely to uncover evidence of criminal activity by the target. Rather, they required only a certification by the government that the information sought was likely to be relevant to a criminal investigation. Section 206 of the act permitted the government to authorize "roving" electronic surveillance, which could be carried out in any location and with any equipment.

In 2015, the USA Freedom Act was passed by Congress and signed into law by President Barack Obama. This law restored and revised through the end of 2019 some provisions of the PATRIOT Act that had recently expired. For example, the USA Freedom Act set limits on the collection of US citizens' telecommunications data by US intelligence agencies, particularly the National Security Agency.

Bush signed the USA PATRIOT Act on October 26, 2001. The act gave law enforcement new powers to investigate terrorism.

law-enforcement agencies wide powers of search and surveillance in terrorism cases.

In January 2002, Bush secretly authorized the National Security Agency (NSA) to monitor the international telephone calls and email messages of American citizens and others in the United States without first obtaining an order from the Foreign Intelligence Surveillance Court, as required by the Foreign Intelligence Surveillance Act of 1978. When the program was revealed in news reports in December 2005, the administration insisted that it was justified by a September 2001 joint Congressional resolution that authorized the president to use "all necessary and appropriate force" against those responsible for the September 11 attacks.

Gitmo and the Treatment of Detainees

The Guantánamo Bay detention camp, often called Gitmo, is a US facility located on the Guantánamo Bay Naval Base in southeastern Cuba. Gitmo, constructed in stages beginning in 2002, was used to house Muslim militants and suspected terrorists captured by US forces in Afghanistan, Iraq, and elsewhere.

In early 2002, the camp began receiving suspected members of al-Qaeda and captured Taliban fighters. Eventually, hundreds of prisoners from several countries were imprisoned there without charge and without the legal means to challenge their detentions. The Bush administration maintained that it was not required to grant basic constitutional protections to the prisoners because the base was outside US territory. It also said that it was not required to observe the Geneva Conventions regarding the humane treatment of prisoners of war and civilians during wartime because the conventions did not apply to what the administration called "unlawful enemy combatants." This term referred to people who fought against the United States or its allies without being part of a regular military force of another country. The administration further maintained that the president had the authority to place any individual, including a US citizen, in indefinite military custody without charge by declaring that person an enemy combatant.

Gitmo became the focus of worldwide controversy in June 2004, after the leak of a confidential report by the International Committee of the Red Cross. The report condemned the camp for alleged human rights violations, including the use of torture during interrogations. The leak of the report came just two months after the publication of photographs of abusive treatment of prisoners by US soldiers at Abu Ghraib prison in Iraq. In response to these revelations, Congress passed the Detainee Treatment Act, which banned the "cruel, inhuman, or degrading" treatment of prisoners in US military custody.

CHAPTER 4

The Iraq War and Other Foreign Affairs

In September 2002, Bush announced a new national security strategy that emphasized the need to defend against terrorists and "rogue states" that might threaten the country with "weapons of mass destruction" (WMD)—biological, chemical, or nuclear arms. In a significant departure from past policy, the strategy declared that the country would take "preemptive" military action to prevent possible attacks. This position put the United States in conflict with much of the international community, especially most of Europe. Critics of the preventive "first-strike" policy argued that it advocated acts of war that could violate international law. They also warned that it set a dangerous precedent for countries that might invoke a perceived threat as justification for military aggression. Bush signaled his intention to put the new strategy into practice by identifying Iraqi president Saddam Hussein as a security threat.

An Ultimatum to Saddam

In late 2002, Bush accused the Iraqi government of possessing and developing

Weapons of Mass Destruction

A weapon of mass destruction (WMD) is a weapon with the capacity to cause death and destruction on such a massive scale and so indiscriminately that its very presence in the hands of a hostile power can be considered a serious threat. A modern WMD is either a nuclear, biological, or chemical weapon. Nuclear weapons release nuclear energy in an explosive manner capable of destroying entire cities. Biological weapons contain natural toxins or infectious agents such as bacteria, viruses, or fungi that are sprayed or burst over populated areas. Chemical weapons consist of liquids and gases that choke their victims, poison their blood, blister their skin, or disrupt their nervous system. Because of the relative ease with which both biological and chemical agents can be prepared, packaged, delivered, and set off, it is feared that they might become the weapon of choice of terrorists.

In February 2003, Secretary of State Colin Powell (*center*) addressed the UN Security Council and offered satellite photographs and intelligence reports that he said provided "irrefutable and undeniable" evidence that Iraq concealed weapons of mass destruction.

WMD in violation of resolutions of the United Nations (UN) Security Council. In October 2002, the US Congress passed a resolution authorizing Bush to use military force in Iraq. In November, the administration successfully lobbied the UN Security Council for a new resolution to send weapons inspectors to Iraq. In December, however, Bush declared that Saddam had failed to comply fully with the new resolution and that Iraq continued to possess weapons of mass destruction.

The United States and its main ally in the affair, the United Kingdom, tried unsuccessfully for several weeks to gain support from other Security Council members for a resolution that explicitly authorized military action against Iraq. France and Russia, while agreeing that Iraq had failed to cooperate fully with weapons inspectors, argued that the inspections regime should be continued and strengthened. As part of the administration's diplomatic campaign, Bush and other officials frequently warned that Iraq possessed WMD, that it was attempting to acquire nuclear weapons, and that it had long-standing ties to al-Qaeda and other terrorist organizations.

Bush declared an end to diplomacy on March 17, 2003, and gave Saddam an ultimatum: he had forty-eight hours to step down and leave Iraq or face removal by force. Saddam refused to leave.

US and Coalition Forces Attack

Bush ordered an invasion of Iraq, which began on March 20 (Iraqi time). The invasion was called Operation Iraqi Freedom.

By mid-April, a coalition of mainly US and British forces had entered all major Iraqi cities and overthrown Saddam's regime. Iraqi guerrilla attacks continued, however, and coalition forces lost control of many areas of the country. Meanwhile, investigations failed to produce evidence to support the administration's claims that Saddam had been developing WMD on a large scale.

As the search for banned weapons continued without success into the following year, Bush's critics accused the administration of having misled the country into war

Coalition forces target Baghdad, Iraq, with missiles in March 2003. The mission to overthrow Saddam Hussein's regime in Iraq was called Operation Iraqi Freedom.

by exaggerating the threat posed by Iraq. In 2004, the Iraq Survey Group, a fact-finding mission composed of US and British experts, concluded that Iraq did not possess WMD or the capacity to produce them at the time of the invasion, though it found evidence that Saddam had planned to reconstitute programs for producing such weapons once UN sanctions were lifted. In the same year, the bipartisan 9-11 Commission (the National Commission on Terrorist Attacks Upon the United States) reported that there was no evidence of a "collaborative operational relationship" between Iraq and al-Qaeda. Saddam, who went into hiding during the invasion, was captured by US forces in December 2003 and was executed by the new Iraqi government three years later.

Occupation and Continued Warfare

Although the Bush administration had planned for a short war, stabilizing the country after the invasion proved difficult. Widespread sectarian violence, accompanied by regular and increasingly deadly attacks on military, police, and civilian targets by militias and terrorist organizations, made large parts of the country virtually ungovernable. The increasing numbers of US dead and wounded, the failure to uncover WMD, and the enormous cost to US taxpayers (approximately $10 billion per month through 2007) gradually eroded public support for the war. By 2005, a clear majority of Americans believed that the Iraq War had been a mistake. By the fifth anniversary of Operation Iraqi Freedom in March 2008, some four thousand US soldiers had been killed. As the death toll mounted, Bush's public-approval

US soldiers carefully approach a building in Samarra, Iraq, in 2004. Coalition forces failed to uncover WMD in Iraq. In January 2005, the search for WMD in that country was called off.

Antiwar protesters demonstrate in New York City. As the number of US soldiers killed in Iraq grew, President Bush's public-approval ratings plummeted.

ratings dropped, falling below 30 percent in many polls.

The President's Emergency Plan for AIDS Relief

Despite the focus on the Iraq War and other issues of national security, President Bush recognized that the United States had an obligation "to make the world better" in addition to making it safer, as he stated in his January 2003 State of the Union address before Congress. He proposed a program to help fifteen countries in Africa and the Caribbean combat the HIV/AIDS pandemic. With a budget of $15 billion over a five-year period, the program, called the President's Emergency Plan for AIDS Relief (PEPFAR), aimed to supply life-extending medications to two million victims of HIV/AIDS, to prevent seven million new cases of the disease, and to provide care for ten million AIDS sufferers and the orphaned children of AIDS victims. This program was widely praised in the United States, even by Bush's critics. It generated enormous goodwill toward the Bush administration in Africa. Medical professionals and public health officials welcomed the greater availability of beneficial drugs but generally objected to the program's requirement that one-third of prevention funds be spent on teaching chastity and fidelity in marriage.

According to PEPFAR's 2016 Annual Report to Congress, in 2015 alone, more than sixty-eight million people were tested for HIV and counseled about HIV prevention, treatment, and care.

CHAPTER 5

Reelection and Domestic Challenges

In 2004, Bush focused his energies on his campaign for reelection against his Democratic challenger, Senator John Kerry of Massachusetts. Bush de-emphasized the economy and instead focused on national security, often invoking the September 11 terrorist attacks.

THE 2004 ELECTION

Bush's key campaign platform during the presidential race was his conduct of the war on terrorism, which he linked with the war in Iraq. Senator Kerry countered that the Iraq War had been poorly planned and executed. Issues of contention included the lack of evidence that Iraq had stocks of WMD (a rationale given for the invasion) and the continuing American casualties in the war. Kerry also insisted that Bush had neglected domestic priorities. He put forth plans to reduce joblessness and the national deficit and to increase access to health care. He also promised to roll back tax cuts that Bush had secured for wealthy citizens. Bush defeated Kerry with slim majorities in the

(*From left to right*) President Bush, Laura Bush, Lynne Cheney, and Vice President Dick Cheney appear at the Republican National Convention in New York City in September 2004. Bush's reelection campaign focused on the war against terrorism.

popular and electoral votes, winning 50.7 percent of the popular vote and 286 electoral votes.

Condoleezza Rice was secretary of state during Bush's second term. She was a fierce defender of his national and foreign policies.

Cabinet Changes

The debate over national security also played a role in the highest profile Cabinet changes at the start of Bush's second term. Secretary of State Colin Powell announced his resignation shortly after Bush's reelection. A political moderate in an administration of hard-liners, Powell had seen his influence in the White House decline as he publicly admitted flaws in the administration's rationale for the Iraq War. He was succeeded by National Security Adviser Condoleezza Rice, a staunch defender of the president's policies. Attorney General John Ashcroft, widely criticized by civil liberties advocates for his zealous enforcement of

Condoleezza Rice

Condoleezza Rice was the first woman and the first African American national security adviser in the United States, serving from 2001 to 2005 under President Bush. She became secretary of state in 2005, during Bush's second term.

Rice was born on November 14, 1954, in Birmingham, Alabama. As an undergraduate, she attended the University of Denver and initially considered becoming a concert pianist. She eventually changed her major to political science, receiving a bachelor's degree in 1974. She earned a master's degree in economics from the University of Notre Dame in 1975 and a doctorate in international studies, with a focus on eastern and central Europe and the Soviet Union, from the University of Denver in 1981. During the early 1980s, she conducted research and taught at Stanford University.

With a growing reputation as an expert on Soviet-bloc politics, in 1986 Rice became an adviser to the Joint Chiefs of Staff under President Ronald Reagan. During the administration of President George H. W. Bush, she was director and then senior director of Soviet and East European affairs on the National Security Council and a special assistant to the president. Rice returned to Stanford in 1991 and served as its provost from 1993 to 1999.

In 1999, Rice left Stanford to become foreign policy adviser to the presidential campaign of George W. Bush. Upon his becoming president, Bush made her national security adviser. After the terrorist attacks of September 11, 2001, Rice supported the US-led attacks on terrorist and Taliban targets in Afghanistan. She also advocated the overthrow of Iraqi president Saddam Hussein. When the administration drew criticism for the Iraq War, Rice strongly defended the president's policies.

As secretary of state, Rice brokered negotiations to end Israel's occupation of the Gaza Strip and led the US effort to promote peace between Israel and the Palestinians. She also persuaded North Korea to return to talks in which that country eventually agreed to dismantle its nuclear weapons program. In addition, Rice called for sanctions against Iran after that country did not end its nuclear program or allow inspections of its nuclear facilities. At the end of the Bush presidency in 2009, Rice returned to her academic career at Stanford. She also became a founding partner at a consulting firm, RiceHadleyGates, LLC.

the USA PATRIOT Act, resigned and was succeeded by Alberto Gonzales. In 2007, Gonzales, too, would resign amid criticism of his handling of the Justice Department.

Social Security and Immigration

The major domestic initiative of Bush's second term was his proposal to replace Social Security (the country's system of government-managed retirement insurance) with private retirement savings accounts. The measure attracted little support, however, mainly because it would have required significant cuts in retirement benefits and heavy borrowing during the transition to the private system.

Bush also proposed a reform of immigration laws that would have allowed most of the estimated twelve million people living in the country illegally to remain temporarily as "guest workers" and to apply for US citizenship after returning to their home countries and paying a fine (though citizenship would not be guaranteed). Although the proposal was supported by some prominent Democrats, including Senator Edward M. Kennedy of

Massachusetts, most other Democrats and many members of Bush's own party remained wary of the idea. Some conservative critics denounced the program as an amnesty that would encourage a new wave of illegal immigration. Liberal opponents warned that it would create a permanent underclass of poor and disenfranchised workers. More than two years of debate produced no reform legislation, though Bush did sign a measure that authorized the construction of a 700-mile (1,127-kilometer) fence along the US-Mexican border.

A border patrol agent guards a spot along the US-Mexican border in Arizona. In 2006, Bush signed a bill to build a fence along part of the border in an effort to reduce the influx of illegal immigrants into the United States.

Environmental and Science Policy

The Bush administration's environmental policies reflected its conviction that economic development could be accomplished without serious harm to the environment. In addition, limits on development, where necessary, should be achieved through voluntary cooperation by industry rather than regulation by government.

After the Supreme Court ruled in April 2007 that greenhouse gas emissions by automobiles constitute a form of air pollution under the Clean Air Act, Bush signed energy legislation that imposed increases in automobile fuel economy standards by the year 2020. In December, however, the Environmental Protection Agency blocked a proposal by California and sixteen other states to issue regulations that would have required fuel economies greater than those called for in the new federal law.

The Bush administration was frequently accused of politically motivated interference in government scientific research. Critics charged that political appointees at various agencies, many of whom had little or no relevant expertise, altered or suppressed scientific reports that did not promote administration policies, restricted the ability of government experts to speak publicly on certain scientific issues, and limited access to scientific information by policy makers and the public. Numerous complaints by environmental and scientific groups led to Congressional hearings in 2007 on political interference in the work of the Surgeon General of the United States and in research on climate change conducted by the National Aeronautics and Space Administration (NASA). In most cases the administration claimed that the interventions were an appropriate attempt to ensure scientific objectivity or simply a routine exercise of the authority of political appointees.

Hurricane Katrina

In late August 2005, Hurricane Katrina struck the southeastern United States, devastating parts of Louisiana, Mississippi, Alabama, and Florida. The storm and its aftermath claimed more than 1,800 lives, and it ranked as the costliest natural disaster in US history.

New Orleans, where much of the land

An aerial view shows flooding in New Orleans, Louisiana, following Hurricane Katrina in August 2005.

is below sea level, was spared a direct hit. However, the levee system designed to hold back the waters of Lake Pontchartrain and Lake Borgne failed after being overwhelmed by 10 inches (25 centimeters) of rain and Katrina's storm surge. By August 30, a day after landfall, New Orleans was about 80 percent underwater.

Although more than a million people left New Orleans before the storm, tens of thousands of residents were unable to leave or refused to do so. Many local agencies were unable to respond to the crisis, and assistance from the federal government, including the Federal Emergency Management Agency, was slow and ineffective. Without an organized effort to restore order in the city, looting became widespread. Shortages of food and drinking water, combined with a lack of basic sanitation, created a public health emergency. It was not until

Supreme Court Nominees

During his second term, Bush appointed two Supreme Court justices: John G. Roberts Jr. (confirmed as the seventeenth chief justice of the United States in 2005, after the death of Chief Justice William H. Rehnquist), and Samuel A. Alito Jr. (confirmed in 2006 to replace the retiring Justice Sandra Day O'Connor). The appointments increased to four the number of solidly conservative justices on the nine-member Supreme Court.

President Bush shakes the hand of John G. Roberts after announcing his nomination of Roberts for Chief Justice of the Supreme Court in September 2005.

September 2 that an effective military presence was established in the city to restore order. US Army engineers finally pumped the last of the floodwaters out of the city on October 11, 2005, some forty-three days after Katrina made landfall. Ultimately, the storm caused more than $100 billion in damage.

When Katrina struck, President Bush was vacationing at his Crawford, Texas, ranch. He did not return to Washington until August 31, two days into the catastrophe. As his plane flew over the city, he viewed the damage from above. He chose not to visit the ravaged areas immediately, claiming that he did not want his presence to interfere with rescue and recovery operations. His actions created a widespread impression among the American public that he was detached from the disaster. This perception, combined with the botched federal relief effort, had a lasting impact on Bush's reputation.

Bush's Last Year in Office

As Bush entered the final year of his presidency in 2008, the country faced enormous challenges. Although al-Qaeda had been

A US Army helicopter lowers a generator at an outpost in Afghanistan in 2008. The war in Afghanistan continued during Bush's final year in office.

subdued, it had not been destroyed. The United States and its allies continued to fight skirmishes with terrorists and their Taliban supporters in Afghanistan, and the insurgency in Iraq continued to claim US casualties. The surpluses in the federal budget in 2000 and 2001 were a distant memory, as the combined effects of military spending, tax cuts, and slow economic growth produced a series of enormous budget deficits starting in 2003. Later in 2008 the economy was threatened by a severe credit crisis, leading Congress to enact a controversial Bush

A stock trader at the New York Stock Exchange looks shocked as the Dow Jones Industrial Average falls more than 500 points on September 15, 2008. The market collapse was part of a financial crisis that rocked the US economy in 2008.

administration plan to rescue the financial industry with up to $700 billion in government funds.

Despite this effort, however, the economy continued its free fall, and Bush's popularity sank to new lows. In the presidential election of 2008, the association of the Republican candidate, John McCain, with the unpopular policies of the Bush administration helped to propel Democrat Barack Obama to a resounding victory. Bush left office on January 20, 2009, and returned to private life in Texas.

Conclusion

In 2008, officials of Southern Methodist University (SMU) in Dallas, Texas, announced plans for the construction of the George W. Bush Presidential Center. Opened in 2013, the center is home to the George W. Bush Presidential Library and Museum and the George W. Bush Institute, a think tank dedicated to research and policy development in education reform, global health, freedom, and economic growth.

During his retirement, Bush kept a low profile and mostly steered clear of politics.

(*From left to right*) Former presidents Jimmy Carter, Bill Clinton, George H. W. Bush, and George W. Bush, along with President Barack Obama, attend the opening of the George W. Bush Presidential Center in Dallas, Texas, in 2013.

He avoided criticizing his Democratic successor, President Barack Obama. In response to a request from Obama in January 2010, Bush and former president Bill Clinton assumed leadership of private fund-raising efforts in the United States for disaster relief in Haiti, which had been struck by a devastating earthquake earlier that month.

Later in 2010, Bush published the memoir *Decision Points*, in which he defended the Iraq War, stated that he personally approved the waterboarding (a controlled drowning technique that many believe is a method of torture) of a captured member of al-Qaeda, reasserted his belief that waterboarding does not constitute torture, and acknowledged the federal government's slow response to Hurricane Katrina. In 2012, he took up painting, and in 2014, he exhibited some of his portraits of world leaders at the George W. Bush Presidential Library and Museum. In the same year he issued *41: A Portrait of My Father*, a biography of the elder Bush, which he called a "love story."

As Bush navigated private life following the presidency, his reputation among the American public began to rebound from his record-low popularity rating when he left office. At the same time, historians just began the process of evaluating the momentous events of Bush's presidency and his responses to them. As the assessment of the Bush years continues, the lingering consequences of the war on terrorism and the Iraq War will be sure to dominate the discussion of his legacy.

Glossary

al-Qaeda Meaning "the Base" in Arabic, al-Qaeda is a terrorist group that was founded by Osama bin Laden in the late 1980s.

amnesty A decision that a group of people will not be punished or that a group of prisoners will be allowed to go free.

antiballistic missile A weapon for intercepting and destroying a ballistic missile, which is a rocket-propelled guided missile.

bioterrorism Terrorism involving the use of biological weapons, which use disease-producing agents such as bacteria, chemicals, viruses, or toxins.

coalition A group of people, groups, or countries that have joined together for a common purpose.

conservative Believing in the value of established and traditional practices in politics and society.

counterterrorism Actions by governments, military forces, and law enforcement to prevent terrorist attacks and destroy terrorist networks.

deliberation Careful thought or discussion for the purpose of making a decision.

disenfranchised Deprived of a legal right or of some privilege.

Geneva Conventions A series of international agreements signed in Geneva, Switzerland, between 1864 and 1949 concerning the treatment of prisoners of war and of the sick, wounded, and dead in battle.

global warming The recent increase in the world's temperature that is believed to be caused by the increase of certain gases, such as carbon dioxide, in the atmosphere.

insurgency A usually violent attempt to take control of a government; a rebellion or uprising.

jurisdiction The power or right to make judgments about the law and to arrest and punish criminals.

liberal Believing that government should be active in supporting social and political change.

preemptive Done to stop an unwanted act from happening.

proficient Good at doing something; well advanced in an art, occupation, or branch of knowledge.

sectarian Relating to sects—religious groups that are smaller parts of a larger group and whose members all share similar beliefs—and the differences between them.

Taliban A fundamentalist Islamic militant group in Afghanistan.

think tank An organization that consists of a group of people who think of new ideas on a particular subject or who give advice about what should be done.

unilateral Involving only one group or country.

For More Information

American Historical Association (AHA)
400 A Street SE
Washington, DC 20003
(202) 544-2422
Website: http://www.historians.org
A professional organization, the AHA promotes the study of history and teaching history as a career. It awards fellowships and grants, and produces a number of publications in the field of history.

George W. Bush Presidential Library and Museum
2943 SMU Boulevard
Dallas, TX 75205
(214) 346-1650
Website: https://www.georgewbushlibrary.smu.edu

The George W. Bush Presidential Library and Museum provides access to presidential papers, records, photographs, videos, and presidential gifts, among other materials that pertain to the presidency of George W. Bush.

National Archives and Records Administration (NARA)
8601 Adelphi Road
College Park, MD 20740-6001
(866) 272-6272
Website: http://www.archives.gov
NARA is an independent government agency that preserves and documents governmental and historical papers and records, including acts of Congress, presidential proclamations, executive orders, and US regulations. Its website contains searchable databases of US historical documents, photos, and veterans' service records. NARA also oversees the presidential library system.

National Museum of American History (NMAH)
1400 Constitution Avenue NW
Washington, DC 20560

(202) 633-1000
Website: http://americanhistory.si.edu
The NMAH has a collection of more than three million artifacts of American history and exhibits many of them. It offers the public information about all aspects of American history and the events that helped shape the American nation. The exhibit "The American Presidency: A Glorious Burden" (http://americanhistory.si.edu/presidency) profiles US presidents through collections of their personal belongings, campaign materials, and other objects.

Texas State Library and Archives Commission
PO Box 12927
Austin, TX 78711
(512) 463-5455
Website: https://www.tsl.texas.gov
The Texas State Library and Archives preserves books, records, maps, and other materials for people who wish to study Texas history and culture. Its website offers information about the tenure of Texas governors, including George W. Bush (https://www.tsl.texas.gov/governors/modern/page3.html#Bush).

The White House
1600 Pennsylvania Avenue NW
Washington, DC 20500
(202) 456-1111
Website: https://www.whitehouse.gov
The White House is the executive mansion where the presidents and their families reside. The White House website provides information about the history of the building, the first ladies, and the presidents, including George W. Bush (https://www.whitehouse.gov/1600/presidents/georgewbush).

Websites

Because of the changing nature of internet links, Rosen Publishing has developed an online list of websites related to the subject of this book. This site is updated regularly. Please use this link to access the list:

http://www.rosenlinks.com/PPPL/wbush

For Further Reading

Brown, Don. *Drowned City: Hurricane Katrina & New Orleans*. New York, NY: Houghton Mifflin Harcourt, 2015.

Bush, George W. *Decision Points*. New York, NY: Crown Publishers, 2010.

Carlisle, Rodney P. *Afghanistan War* (America at War). New York, NY: Chelsea House Publishers, 2010.

Carlisle, Rodney P. *Iraq War* (America at War). Rev. ed. New York, NY: Chelsea House Publishers, 2010.

Freed, Kira. *Surviving Hurricane Katrina* (Surviving Disaster). New York, NY: Rosen Publishing, 2016.

Greene, John Robert. *The George W. Bush Years*. New York, NY: Facts On File, 2011.

Heppermann, Christine. *Bush v. Gore: The Florida Recounts of the 2000 Presidential Election* (Landmark Supreme Court

Cases). Minneapolis, MN: ABDO Publishing, 2013.

Hillstrom, Kevin. *The September 11 Terrorist Attacks*. Detroit, MI: Omnigraphics, 2012.

Hollar, Sherman, ed. *Barack Obama* (Pivotal Presidents: Profiles in Leadership). New York, NY: Britannica Educational Publishing, 2013.

Kelley, Donald R., and Todd G. Shields, eds. *Taking the Measure: The Presidency of George W. Bush*. College Station, TX: Texas A&M University Press, 2013.

Lansford, Tom, and Robert P. Watson, eds. *George W. Bush* (Presidents and Their Decisions). Detroit, MI: Greenhaven Press, 2005.

Lee, Sally. *George W. Bush*. North Mankato, MN: Capstone Press, 2013.

Lowery, Zoe, ed. *Key Figures of the Wars in Iraq and Afghanistan* (Biographies of War). New York, NY: Britannica Educational Publishing, 2016.

Mann, Jim. *George W. Bush*. New York, NY: Times Books/Henry Holt and Company, 2015.

Sherman, Patrice. *George W. Bush: Texas Governor and U.S. President*. Huntington

Beach, CA: Teacher Created Materials, 2013.

Stefoff, Rebecca. *The Patriot Act* (Landmark Legislation). New York, NY: Marshall Cavendish Benchmark, 2011.

Wilson, Mike. *Terrorism* (Opposing Viewpoints). Detroit, MI: Greenhaven Press, 2009.

Wolny, Philip. *Iran and Iraq: Religion, War, and Geopolitics.* New York, NY: Rosen Publishing, 2010.

Index

A

B

C

D

E

F

G

H

I

J

K

M

N

O

P

R

S

T

U

W

Y